RESTORED GROUND

Unapologetically Unbound: Reclaiming Who You Are in Christ

Marcia Jerry

Above All Cost

Published by: Above All Cost

Paperback ISBN: 979-8-9946574-0-9

Printed in the United States of America.

This book is for inspirational and educational purposes only and is not intended to replace professional counseling, therapy, medical or legal advice. If you are experiencing abuse, severe emotional distress, or are in an unsafe situation, please seek immediate professional support.

DEDICATION

Dedicated to the amazing love of my life and best friend, my husband. To my daughter, who always chooses to rise above adversity. And to all who dared to believe that healing is possible.

Acknowledgments

First and always, I give honor and praise to God, the Lord over my life. This book exists because of His grace, His patience, and His relentless love. He met me in places I did not think I could be restored from, and He continues to lead me in truth, healing, and purpose.

I am deeply grateful for my family, whose love, support, and prayers have carried me through every season. Thank you for your encouragement, your patience, and for believing in what God placed in my heart.

I also extend heartfelt thanks to my pastors, Pastor Eric Hallback and Pastor Yaisa Hallback. Thank you for your leadership, your obedience to God's call, and for faithfully pouring into my life. Your guidance, prayers, and example of walking in truth and love have helped shape both my faith and this work.

To everyone who has prayed, encouraged, listened, and supported this journey, thank you. May God receive all the glory.

TABLE OF CONTENTS

Introduction

Restored Ground — Where Healing Begins

We are born into this world without choosing many of the things that shape our beginning, our families, our environments, or the circumstances we first step into. Yet as life unfolds, one of the areas where we do have a choice is in the relationships we choose to begin, maintain, or end. Those choices matter. They shape how we see ourselves, how we allow others to treat us, and often, how we understand God.

Relationships can be simple and complex all at once. But before we can truly cultivate healthy relationships with others, it is essential to examine the relationship we have with ourselves. How we see ourselves, our worth, our boundaries, our expectations, either positions us for freedom or entangles us in patterns that bring harm. We are accustomed to quick exchanges: "How are you?" "Good." Yet how often is that answer true? How often do we quietly carry hurt, confusion, or exhaustion beneath the surface, convincing ourselves that we are "fine" when something inside us is longing to be seen and healed?

So let me ask you questions many of us rarely consider:

- How is your relationship with yourself?
- Do you make space to evaluate your own emotions?
- Do you speak to yourself with compassion or criticism?
- Are your expectations rooted in truth, or shaped by fear, familiarity, and past wounds?

Often, we pour into others while neglecting ourselves. And sometimes, we place our relationship with God at the bottom of the list as well. Yet these relationships are deeply connected. When we nurture our relationship with God, we begin to see ourselves more clearly. And as our understanding of ourselves grows, we become more discerning in the relationships we form and maintain. How we treat ourselves quietly teaches others how to treat us.

Many of us remain in unhealthy relationships not because we are weak, but because fear quietly influences what feels normal. Fear of change. Fear of being alone. Fear of not being enough. Fear of facing reality. Over time, fear blurs our vision, reshapes our standards, and convinces us to settle where God is calling us to rise.

Scripture reminds us that fear does not come from God. Yet fear often becomes the unspoken force behind our choices. It keeps us bound to patterns that wound us and distanced from the freedom God desires for us.

No matter how complex or painful our stories may be, God still desires relationship with us. He meets us where we are, but He does not intend to leave us there.

I have personally discovered that some of the places I found myself reflected how I once saw myself and what I believed I deserved. It was through discovering who I am in Christ that my understanding began to change. God is not afraid to meet us in broken places, but He lovingly invites us to be transformed there.

Psalm 36:9 says, "For with you is the fountain of life; in your light we see light." God is the source of life and clarity. As we grow in relationship with Him, He reveals truth, restores identity, and teaches us how to build healthier relationships, with ourselves, with others, and with Him.

Restored Ground is an invitation into that process. It is a starting place, a space to confront fear, examine patterns, and realign your life with Christ. Through the themes of Familiar, Enough, Alone, and Reality, this book invites you to explore the beliefs and behaviors that shape your relationships and to discover the freedom that emerges when truth and grace meet.

If you are ready to step onto new ground, to be honest about what has been, and to open your heart to what God desires to rebuild, this journey is for you.

Familiar

Breaking Free from What Feels Normal but Isn't Healthy

Familiar

Over time, people and environments become familiar to us, especially family members, close friends, or long-standing relationships. Familiarity creates patterns of regularity in our lives, and those patterns quietly shape our expectations. These expectations may be rooted in healthy principles, or they may be built on unhealthy standards. The problem arises when what feels normal is no longer what is healthy.

When familiarity is rooted in dysfunction, we begin to justify behaviors and circumstances that should give us pause. We say things like, "That's just the way they are," "This is how I was raised," "It will always be like this," "I can't help it," or "You make me act this way." Over time, unhealthy familiarity can form a cycle that is difficult to break and damaging to both us and others.

Continual exposure to unhealthy people or toxic situations distorts our perception. What once felt unacceptable slowly begins to feel normal. Our internal filters adjust. Our standards shift. When unhealthy familiarity goes unchallenged, it begins to infringe on our identity and the way we see ourselves.

It is important to clarify that familiarity itself is not inherently negative. There is comfort in the familiar, the smell of a home-cooked meal, returning to a meaningful place, or revisiting memories that bring warmth and peace. These forms of familiarity can be grounding and life-giving. However, in this section, we are addressing the kind of familiarity that binds us to unhealthy relationships, patterns, and environments.

If a relationship causes physical, emotional, mental, or financial harm, it warrants honest evaluation. We must ask difficult but necessary questions: Why do I find this acceptable? Why do I feel compelled to settle for this treatment? These are not healthy relationship pathways, and we should not become comfortable enduring what slowly diminishes us.

Scripture shows us that familiarity can become a trap when fear convinces us to return to what is known rather than trust God for what He has promised.

We see this clearly in the story of the Israelites. God promised to lead them into a land flowing with milk and honey. Moses sent spies into the land of Canaan to explore it. They confirmed that the land was good and abundant, but they also saw that it was already inhabited. Fear took hold of many of the spies, and they allowed insecurity and self-doubt to overshadow God's promise. Their report stirred fear and division among the people.

Joshua and Caleb spoke differently. They acknowledged the presence of obstacles, but they trusted God's promise and believed He would give them victory. They attempted to call the people out of fear and into faith. Yet the people, overwhelmed by uncertainty, longed to return to Egypt. They preferred the familiarity of bondage over the uncertainty of freedom.

The Israelites forgot what they had been delivered from. Slavery, hardship, and oppression faded from memory, replaced by discomfort and fear of the unknown. They overlooked the miracles, manna from heaven, water from rocks, and God's continual provision. What they wanted to return to was not what was best for them.

Like the Israelites, we can find ourselves drawn back to unhealthy familiarity simply because it feels known. When something or someone causes ongoing pain and prevents growth, why do we feel compelled to stay, or even return? If we recognize a situation is harmful and we leave, why do we bind ourselves to it again? Fear can blind us, distort truth, and keep us in bondage if we are not careful.

Moving beyond unhealthy familiarity requires faith. It means stepping into discomfort and trusting God through the unknown. We must slow down, seek God's guidance, and resist leaning on our own understanding. God desires relationship with us, and discernment grows through time spent with Him in prayer, Scripture, trust, and obedience. We may be in the driver's seat, but God provides the direction. We can choose to follow His lead or continue navigating on our own.

God ultimately brought those who trusted Him into the promised land. And while God meets us wherever we are, even when our own choices lead us into difficult places, He also invites us to move forward. He can lead us out of unhealthy familiarity and into new beginnings, hope, and a future (Jeremiah 29:11). But it begins with our willingness to open the door and trust Him.

Breaking free from unhealthy familiarity requires courage. It means setting new standards for what is acceptable in our lives. As we grow and gain perspective, our lenses become clearer and our hearts more discerning. We learn to recognize warning signs, believe patterns when they appear, and walk away from what tears us down. Forgive yourself for staying too long. Growth brings wisdom, and wisdom brings change.

Do not remain stuck simply because something feels familiar. Examine your relationships honestly. Pray for clarity. Ask God for direction. Trust Him enough to move forward.

Breaking free from unhealthy familiarity requires more than recognizing harmful patterns. It requires understanding why we stayed. Often, what keeps us bound is not only what feels familiar, but what we believe about our own worth. When our sense of value is distorted, we tolerate what we should not.

To move forward, we must confront the question beneath the patterns, the question that shapes our choices, our boundaries, and our relationships:

Am I enough?

As we turn to Scripture, may God begin to speak truth where fear and familiarity once defined us.

Familiar Scripture Reflection

As you reflect on what you have read, allow these Scriptures to remind you that God is with you as you step away from what is familiar and into what He is doing new. Read slowly. Pause often. Let His truth guide and strengthen your heart.

Hebrews 11:11

And by faith even Sarah, who was past childbearing age, was enabled to bear children because she considered him faithful who had made the promise.

Proverbs 3:5–6

Trust in the Lord with all your heart and lean not on your own understanding; in all your ways submit to him, and he will make your paths straight.

Joshua 1:9

Have I not commanded you? Be strong and courageous. Do not be afraid; do not be discouraged, for the Lord your God will be with you wherever you go.

Isaiah 41:10

So do not fear, for I am with you; do not be dismayed, for I am your God. I will strengthen you and help you; I will uphold you with my righteous right hand.

Isaiah 43:18–19

Forget the former things; do not dwell on the past. See, I am doing a new thing Now it springs up; do you not perceive it? I am making a way in the wilderness and streams in the wasteland.

2 Corinthians 5:17

Therefore, if anyone is in Christ, the new creation has come: The old has gone, the new is here!

Philippians 4:6–7

Do not be anxious about anything, but in every situation, by prayer and petition, with thanksgiving, present your requests to God. And the peace of God, which transcends all understanding, will guard your hearts and your minds in Christ Jesus.

Psalm 147:3

He heals the brokenhearted and binds up their wounds.

Take a moment to sit with what God has revealed before moving forward.

Enough

Reclaiming Identity, Worth, and God's Truth About You

Enough

Have you ever struggled with the feeling of not being good enough? Have you ever questioned your purpose or wrestled with feelings of inadequacy? Often, these emotions have little to do with our actual performance and far more to do with our sense of worth. When they are coupled with unhealthy relationships, they become magnified. This is why it is essential to know not only who you are, but whose you are.

In a society dominated by expectations, living authentically can feel nearly impossible. Yet the journey toward understanding your identity is critical. If you do not define who you are, someone else will, and if you are not careful, you may begin to believe them. External pressures and internal insecurities often manifest as feelings of inadequacy or worthlessness. These pressures may stem from career demands, parenting responsibilities, or relational dynamics. A healthy sense of self is foundational to forming healthy, meaningful relationships. There is freedom in being yourself unapologetically rather than living within the confines of who others expect you to be. Feelings of inadequacy can cloud our judgment, but the truth remains: we are more than enough.

Maya Angelou once said, "I've learned that people will forget what you've said, people will forget what you did, but they will never forget the way you make them feel." A glance, a gesture, or a single sentence can shake us to the core. The saying "sticks and stones may break my bones, but words will never hurt me" is simply not true. Words do hurt, and hurt people often hurt others. Unfortunately, those closest to us frequently know exactly what to say and how to say it in ways that cut deeply.

Healing begins when we reach a place where the words or actions of others no longer define us. Breaking free from toxic relationships starts with self-reflection and a willingness to truly know yourself. When you understand your worth, you become better equipped to navigate negativity without internalizing it. While harmful words or actions may still occur, they no longer determine your identity. Freedom is sustained through establishing and maintaining healthy boundaries.

Before absorbing the opinions, emotions, or accusations placed on you by others, pause and reflect. Ask yourself: Is there truth in what is being said? Consider the source. What kind of fruit is evident in their life? What is their intent, to build you up or to tear you down? Do they genuinely have your best interest at heart? Are they qualified to speak into your life? And finally, is there something God may be inviting you to address or grow in? Discernment allows us to move forward in purpose rather than remain trapped by misplaced voices.

Bernice Johnson Reagon wisely said, “Life’s challenges are not supposed to paralyze you; they’re supposed to help you discover who you are.” Imperfection is part of the human experience. Regardless of what you have faced, extend grace to yourself and continue moving forward. Your worth is not determined by how others treat you, and your adequacy is not dictated by past failures or present emotions.

Scripture reminds us that our worth is not found in performance or approval, but in our identity in Christ, whose grace is sufficient and whose love defines us. Psalm 30:11 declares, “You turned my wailing into dancing; you removed my sackcloth and clothed me with joy.” This verse reveals a powerful truth: God does not ignore pain; He transforms it.

Throughout Scripture, we see this pattern of divine reversal again and again. What others intend for harm; God redeems for good. What the enemy seeks to use for defeat, God turns into deliverance. Joseph’s betrayal led to preservation (Genesis 50:20). Oppression gave way to freedom (Exodus 1–2). Mourning was turned into victory for God’s people (Esther 9:1). Death was defeated through resurrection (Acts 2:23–24). Divine reversal is the unseen hand of God at work, turning mourning into joy, weakness into strength, and inadequacy into purpose. Through Christ, we are not defined by what we lack, but by what He supplies. In Him, we are more than enough.

Knowing who you are is deeply connected to knowing whose you are. You were created with intention and loved before you ever took a breath. No matter how you see yourself, or struggle to see yourself, God chooses you every time. His grace is sufficient, and when you enter into relationship with Him, He begins to reveal your identity and purpose. This journey is not about conforming to others' expectations or allowing yourself to be shaped by unhealthy influences. God is faithful and truthful, and even when the truth is difficult to accept, He remains present. He will never leave you nor forsake you, and He will walk with you through every season.

When you develop a relationship with Jesus, He teaches you how to love and forgive yourself, and how to extend that same grace to others. He sharpens your discernment, helping you recognize intentions and warning signs. God always provides a way out, but we must remain attentive and willing to respond. Forgiveness is often one of the most difficult steps in healing, yet it is also one of the most freeing. Unforgiveness is a trap; it slowly consumes us from within, and if left unaddressed, seeps into every area of our lives.

Jesus exemplifies forgiveness perfectly. He entered an imperfect world, was betrayed and abandoned, and yet even while suffering on the cross, He prayed, "Father, forgive them, for they do not know what they are doing." Though you may feel undeserving or inadequate, God declares otherwise. We are forgiven, and in turn, we are called to forgive.

Through relationship with God, we find peace, and from that place of peace, we can begin forgiving ourselves and others.

A relationship with God is like having a Father, a best friend, and a guide all in one: Father, Son, and Holy Spirit. It is not about rigid rules or rituals, but about connection, vulnerability, and trust. Through prayer, reflection, and daily communication with God, we gain clarity, peace, and direction. As we learn to listen, to the gentle nudges, signs, and truths He reveals, we grow in spiritual strength and self-awareness. From this place of wholeness, we develop healthier relationships and gain the courage to distance ourselves from those that are toxic or harmful.

Learning that our worth is secure in Christ reshapes how we relate to others, but it also reshapes how we relate to ourselves. When external validation no longer defines us, we are invited into something deeper: the ability to be still, whole, and grounded in God's presence.

Sometimes, healing requires learning how to be alone without fear.

As we turn to Scripture, may God continue to affirm the truth of who you are and gently lead you into wholeness.

Enough Scripture Reflection

Let these Scriptures speak to your worth, your identity, and God's unchanging love for you. As you read, allow His Word to replace every lie with truth and every doubt with the assurance of who you are in Christ.

2 Corinthians 12:9

But he said to me, "My grace is sufficient for you, for my strength is made perfect in weakness." Therefore I will boast all the more gladly about my weaknesses, so that Christ's power may rest on me.

Psalm 139:13–14

For you created my inmost being; you knit me together in my mother's womb. I praise you because I am fearfully and wonderfully made; your works are wonderful, I know that full well.

Ephesians 2:10

For we are God's handiwork, created in Christ Jesus to do good works, which God prepared in advance for us to do.

1 Peter 2:9

But you are a chosen people, a royal priesthood, a holy nation, God's special possession, that you may declare the praises of him who called you out of darkness into his wonderful light.

Numbers 6:24–26

"The Lord bless you and keep you; the Lord make his face to shine upon you, and be gracious unto you; the Lord lift his countenance upon you, and give you peace.'"

Psalm 40:1–2

I waited patiently for the Lord; he turned to me and heard my cry. He lifted me out of the slimy pit, out of the mud and mire; he set my feet on a rock and gave me a firm place to stand.

Romans 12:2

Do not conform to the pattern of this world, but be transformed by the renewing of your mind. Then you will be able to test and approve what God's will is, his good, pleasing and perfect will.

Deuteronomy 28:13

The Lord will make you the head, not the tail. If you pay attention to the commands of the Lord your God that I give you this day and carefully follow them, you will always be at the top, never at the bottom.

Take a moment to thank God for who He says you are.

Alone

Finding Strength, Clarity, and Healing in God's Presence

Alone

Many people equate being alone with loneliness, vulnerability, or depression, but that is not always the case. While some individuals struggle with solitude, others genuinely enjoy it. The issue is not being alone itself; the issue arises when fear is attached to the idea of being alone, whether relationally or physically.

Nir Eyal notes in Psychology Today that:

- One in three adults report a fear of being alone.
- This fear often causes people to prioritize relationship status over relationship quality, leading to unhealthy partnerships.
- Embracing quality solitude can actually strengthen our relationships.

Moments of solitude or singleness can become powerful seasons of growth. In these quieter spaces, we gain uninterrupted time to think, plan, reflect, and experience restoration. The world is loud and demanding, constantly pulling for our attention and often leaving little room for stillness. Yet stillness is where clarity begins.

If being alone or still brings feelings of anxiety, that discomfort may be revealing unresolved fears that need attention. This is not something to ignore. It may be wise and healthy to seek professional guidance to process what may be emerging internally. When we are not whole, it becomes difficult to show up fully in relationships. We end up offering fragments of ourselves instead of the fullness God desires. How can we pour into others when our own tank is consistently empty?

Throughout Scripture, we see that seasons of intentional solitude often become places of preparation, where God strengthens His people before calling them to act in faith.

Jesus modeled this pattern clearly. He regularly withdrew from crowds, and even from His disciples, to pray and commune with the Father (Mark 1:35; Luke 5:16; John 6:15). These moments of solitude were not signs of weakness or avoidance, but of wisdom and alignment. In solitude, Jesus prayed, reflected, and received direction from God.

We see a similar pattern in the life of Esther. One of the most pivotal moments in her story occurred when she prepared to approach the king, her husband, to reveal her Jewish identity and plead for the lives of her people. This act carried great risk. Before stepping into that moment, Esther called for a time of fasting, positioning herself and others in dependence on God (Esther 4:16). While Scripture does not detail every private moment, it is clear that Esther intentionally sought God's strength and wisdom before acting.

Leaving unhealthy relationships or engaging in difficult conversations, especially those involving boundaries, often requires similar courage, humility, and faith.

Like Esther, we must prepare our hearts before stepping forward. When we seek God sincerely, He provides the wisdom and strength needed to move forward.

Singleness can be a season of healing, rebuilding, and refocusing. It allows space to deepen our relationship with God and to better understand who we are apart from external validation. If you find yourself in a season of singleness, resist the temptation to view it as a deficiency. Instead, see it as an opportunity for restoration and growth.

Do not allow the world, or other people, to define your worth. Everyone will have an opinion, but the most important question remains: Who does God say you are? Are the relationships in your life drawing you closer to who God is calling you to be, or pulling you away from it? Do they encourage growth, or do they diminish it?

In moments of solitude, we reconnect with Jesus, with our true selves, and with what we need to be renewed. As many introverts like to say, time alone helps reset our "people meter." When we regularly refill our cup, we are better equipped to cultivate healthy, life-giving relationships with God, ourselves, and others.

Being okay with being alone is not about isolation; it is about strength. It is the recognition that remaining in unhealthy relationships often costs more than walking away.

As Maya Angelou wisely said, “You may not control all the events that happen to you, but you can decide not to be reduced by them.”

Embracing this mindset requires honesty. It means acknowledging reality and choosing, with God’s guidance, to step away from environments and relationships that diminish us, and instead embrace those that nurture the life He desires for us.

Solitude creates space for clarity. When the noise quiets and we become honest before God, truth begins to surface. Yet clarity also requires courage, the courage to face what is real, not what we wish were true. Healing cannot happen in denial.

To walk forward in freedom, we must be willing to confront reality.

As we turn to Scripture, may God meet you in the quiet, strengthen you in truth, and prepare your heart for what He desires to restore next.

Alone Scripture Reflection

In this quiet space, allow these Scriptures to draw you into the presence of God. As you read, let His Word remind you that you are never alone, that He is near, and that restoration often begins in stillness.

Deuteronomy 31:8

The Lord himself goes before you and will be with you; he will never leave you nor forsake you. Do not be afraid; do not be discouraged.

Isaiah 43:2

When you pass through the waters, I will be with you; and when you pass through the rivers, they will not sweep over you. When you walk through the fire, you will not be burned; the flames will not set you ablaze.

Psalm 23:4

Even though I walk through the darkest valley, I will fear no evil, for you are with me; your rod and your staff, they comfort me.

Psalm 34:18

The Lord is close to the brokenhearted and saves those who are crushed in spirit.

Psalm 62:1–2

Truly my soul finds rest in God; my salvation comes from him. Truly he is my rock and my salvation; he is my fortress, I will never be shaken.

Exodus 14:14

The Lord will fight for you; you need only to be still.

2 Timothy 1:7

For the Spirit God gave us does not make us timid, but gives us power, love and self-discipline.

Ephesians 2:19–22

Consequently, you are no longer foreigners and strangers, but fellow citizens with God's people and also members of his household, [20] built on the foundation of the apostles and prophets, with Christ Jesus himself as the chief cornerstone. In him the whole building is joined together and rises to become a holy temple in the Lord. And in him you too are being built together to become a dwelling in which God lives by his Spirit.

Allow yourself to rest in God's presence before continuing.

Reality

Embracing Truth, Walking in Faith, and Living Renewed

Reality

Imagine writing the perfect narrative for your life. Picture a version where nothing is flawed, where every imperfection is edited out like a filtered image. What would change? Your relationships, your finances, your career, your health, the home you live in, the life you present to the world? Now pause, and return to reality.

Life is not perfect. Relationships are not perfect. People are not perfect. And pretending otherwise only creates false narratives we eventually have to confront. This exercise may feel hypothetical, but many people live this way daily, airbrushing truth to avoid discomfort. As Lauryn Hill once said, the real you is better than the fake someone else. That truth matters.

Reality is this: life can be hard. Seasons can be messy. Yet we are not without hope. While we cannot change yesterday, we are given the opportunity to shape tomorrow by the choices we make today. Complacency keeps us stuck, but truth invites movement. Each new day brings fresh grace and mercy, and with it, the chance to grow. The past does not define you. If something in your life is not aligned with truth, you are not powerless to change it.

False narratives act like a covering, masking what we fear to face. But denial does not heal; truth does. On the other side of hard truth is freedom, growth, and often a powerful testimony. Beauty can come from brokenness when truth is embraced rather than avoided.

In Christ, our identity is made new. Our worth and strength are rooted in Him, not in our circumstances or past failures. We are no longer bound to the expectations others place on us or the labels they attempt to assign. What was once broken is being renewed. What was old no longer defines us.

Through prayer and honest surrender, God opens our eyes to truth and gives us the courage to confront reality without denial. As our relationship with Him deepens, we gain the strength to release relationships and patterns rooted in dysfunction and those that no longer reflect His love, His peace, or His purpose. In doing so, we step into the freedom Christ has already secured for us.

Walking in newness of life does not mean the absence of trials; it means we now face them with faith.

We see this clearly in the story of Shadrach, Meshach, and Abednego. When King Nebuchadnezzar rose to power, he selected young Israelite men who were considered intelligent, capable, and promising, bringing them into service under his rule. They were given new assignments, new education, and even new names.

Though their circumstances changed, their allegiance to God did not.

When the king issued a decree that everyone must bow to the golden image he had set up, Shadrach, Meshach, and Abednego refused. They chose faithfulness over comfort, obedience over approval, and truth over cultural pressure. Because of their stance, they were thrown into a fiery furnace. Yet Scripture tells us that when the king looked into the fire, he saw not three men, but four walking unharmed among the flames (Daniel 3). God was with them in the fire.

Their story reminds us that walking in our new identity does not mean challenges will cease. In Christ we are made new, yet reality remains. Trials will arise, pressures will come, and obedience may still cost us something. But when we know who we are and whose we are, we can walk in courage. God does not promise a life free from hardship, but He does promise His presence in every season.

Walking in faith can sometimes feel like stepping into a furnace or into the unknown. Yet we are called to walk by faith and not by sight. If God is calling you forward, He will sustain you there. Even when we walk through the valley of the shadow of death, we fear no evil, for He is with us (Psalm 23:4). We are not called to conform to the limitations others place on us, but to live anchored in what God has spoken. His Word will never return void.

People may try to remind you of who you used to be, but you are not defined by former seasons, past mistakes, or outdated titles. God calls you redeemed, forgiven, chosen, and free. Keep your eyes forward. Release the weight of yesterday. Let go of false labels and walk confidently into who God says you are becoming.

Scripture reminds us that "you will know the truth, and the truth will set you free" (John 8:32). Embracing reality often requires uncomfortable honesty, repentance, or change, but transformation frequently begins there. Consider Saul, later known as Paul. When confronted with truth on the road to Damascus, he could have resisted or remained the same. Instead, he surrendered, and his life was forever changed.

Growth in Christ requires releasing what no longer aligns with who God is shaping us to become. This includes habits, mindsets, titles, and sometimes relationships that belong to a former season. Do not fear the refining process. God reveals truth not to condemn us, but to redeem us.

Let go of what was. Embrace what is. And step forward in faith into what God is doing next. You are being renewed daily. You are equipped to walk boldly in the life God has prepared for you.

As we turn to Scripture, may God continue to reveal truth, strengthen your steps, and confirm the freedom He is unfolding in your life.

Reality Scripture Reflection

As you move forward, let these Scriptures anchor you in truth and strengthen your faith. May God's Word meet you in what is real, guide your steps, and remind you that He is faithful in every season.

John 8:32

Then you will know the truth, and the truth will set you free.

Psalm 25:5

Guide me in your truth and teach me, for you are God my Savior, and my hope is in you all day long.

Hebrews 11:1

Now faith is confidence in what we hope for and assurance about what we do not see.

2 Corinthians 4:8–9

We are hard pressed on every side but not crushed; perplexed, but not in despair; persecuted, but not abandoned; struck down, but not destroyed.

2 Corinthians 12:9

But he said to me, "My grace is sufficient for you, for my power is made perfect in weakness." Therefore, I will boast all the more gladly about my weaknesses, so that Christ's power may rest on me.

Ephesians 2:8–10

For it is by grace you have been saved, through faith, and this is not from yourselves, it is the gift of God, not by works, so that no one can boast. For we are God's handiwork, created in Christ Jesus to do good works, which God prepared in advance for us to do.

Isaiah 61:7

Instead of your shame you will receive a double portion, and instead of disgrace you will rejoice in your inheritance. And so you will inherit a double portion in your land, and everlasting joy will be yours.

Galatians 6:9

Let us not become weary in doing good, for at the proper time we will reap a harvest if we do not give up.

May God's truth continue to guide you as you walk forward in freedom.

Stepping onto New Ground

You did not arrive here by accident or by chance. Something in you desired understanding, healing, or change, and that willingness to look inward matters.

Throughout this book, you have explored what feels familiar, what has shaped your sense of worth, what loneliness has whispered, and what reality has required you to face. You have examined beliefs, patterns, and relationships that may have once felt normal but were never meant to define you. And in doing so, you have made space for truth to meet you.

Restoration does not begin with perfection. It begins with honesty. With the courage to admit where something is broken, unclear, or unhealthy, and with the humility to invite God into that space. God is not intimidated by your questions, your wounds, or your past. He is drawn to them. Scripture reminds us that He is close to the brokenhearted, that He restores what has been lost, and that He makes all things new.

New ground is rarely comfortable. It often requires releasing what is familiar, even when what is familiar is painful. But new ground is also where freedom grows. It is where identity is rebuilt. It is where truth replaces fear, and where grace becomes the foundation instead of survival. Take hope in knowing that your ground is not only restored, but it is made new!

As you move forward, remember that healing is not linear. Some days will feel strong. Others may feel tender. Both are part of the process. What matters is not how quickly you move, but that you continue to move with God. Stay anchored to His Word. Stay honest in prayer. Stay aware of the patterns you are building. Give yourself permission to grow.

About the Author

Marcia Jerry is a woman of faith, a writer, and the founder of Above All Cost. Her work is rooted in her own journey of healing, restoration, and learning to build healthy relationships through a deeper relationship with God.

Through personal experience, prayer, and study of Scripture, Marcia came to understand how identity, self-worth, and faith are deeply connected to the relationships we choose and the patterns we tolerate. What once were seasons of confusion and brokenness became places where God met her, rebuilt her, and revealed the power of living rooted in truth.

Marcia writes with honesty, compassion, and purpose, creating space for readers to confront unhealthy cycles, rediscover who they are in Christ, and walk forward in freedom. Her heart is to help others recognize toxic patterns, align their lives with God's truth, and develop the courage to set healthy boundaries while embracing restoration.

She believes that no story is wasted, no heart is beyond healing, and no season is too broken for God to restore. Through her writing and the mission of Above All Cost, Marcia seeks to remind others that healing is possible, identity is found in Christ, and freedom begins when we are willing to meet God on restored ground.

www.ingramcontent.com/pod-product-compliance
Lightning Source LLC
LaVergne TN
LVHW011628120826
845149LV00022B/2769